Working Out with the Word of God

Don Matzat

"For physical training is of some value, but godliness has value for all things, holding promise for both the present life and the life to come." (I Timothy 4: 8)

D1533242

Good News Books
O'Fallon, Missouri
Copyright@ 2017 Donald G. Matzat

Table of Contents

Introduction:

Why is it that many Christians do not know the content of the Bible? Some claim not to understand the Bible. Perhaps the problem is they don't know where to begin or how to pursue personal Bible study. For one thing, the Bible is the inspired Word of God. Seeking the Holy Spirit is vital. The Bible also contains a variety of literature. If a person begins in Genesis, by the time he gets to Leviticus he may be bored and lose interest. The singular purpose for a Christian to study the Bible is to get to know Jesus better, to believe in Him, and to use his Word against the temptations and issues of life. For this reason, studying the Bible must be intentional and directed.

Working Out with the Word of God compares studying the Word with physical exercise. Paul writes to Timothy, "For physical training is of some value, but godliness has value for all things, holding promise for both the present life and the life to come." (I Timothy 4: 8)

This little volume is divided into five sections:

1) Do You need Spiritual Exercise?

2) Preparing for Your Workout

3) Meditating upon the Word of God.

4) Setting Your Priorities

5) Where do You Begin?

Hopefully, after reading this, you will be encouraged to dig into the Word of God with a directed intention, methodology, and purpose.

The Author:

Don Matzat has been a pastor in the Lutheran Church-Missouri Synod for over fifty years. He is the author of *Christ-Esteem*, *Truly Transformed*, *Inner Healing: Deliverance or Deception* and *The Lord Told Me: I Think*. He has also authored the novels *Redemption*, *Reconciliation*, and *The Righteous One*. Don and his wife Dianne have been married for fifty-four years. They have four children and eleven grandchildren. Direct any questions to: donmatzat@hotmail.com.

Part 1: Do You Need Spiritual Exercise?

Physical fitness is a very popular theme today. Perhaps many of you have been influenced by the drive to "get into shape." The benefits of entering a physical fitness program are many. You will have a healthier body and probably live longer. You will have more stamina. You will look better, feel better about yourself, and can relate to others with more confidence.

While it is good to be concerned with physical training, it is even better to be concerned with spiritual training. We are not only "physical" beings, but we have a spiritual dimension to our lives. The Christian faith is neither physical nor mental but involves our "spiritual life." Our relationship with Jesus Christ is brought into being by the Holy Spirit and believing in Jesus and living in relationship with Jesus is the essence of the Christian's spiritual life.

The Bible tells us to spiritually exercise or train ourselves. The Apostle Paul tells Timothy that while there is some value to physical training, spiritual training or, as he puts It, "training in godliness" has far greater value, not only for this life, but for the age to come. (I Timothy 4: 8)

11

A Spiritual Age

We are living in a very spiritual age. If you browse through your local secular bookstore, especially in the section labeled "New Age" or "spirituality" you will find a variety of books promoting "spiritual exercises." Many authors offer their "secrets" of spirituality. They promote a variety of practices such as yoga, astrology, Transcendental Meditation, creative visualization, channeling, angels and spirit-guides, supernatural healing, psychic phenomena, and magical arts. New concepts are explained such as mantras, shakras, and karma. New sources of spiritual power are identified such as inner spirit guides, pyramids and crystals.

Even among Christians, strange spiritual exercises are very popular. Some authors encourage Christians to visualize Jesus and talk to him, thus receiving the "word of the Lord." Others speak of their near-death experiences or boast of their visions of and excursions to heaven. Beware of books that speak of "spiritual disciplines," or "spirituality."

The only spiritual exercise that God himself has approved is to "Work out with the Word of God." He has clearly said that all other spiritual exercise programs that do not find their origin in his Word will lead into spiritual darkness and great deception. (Deuteronomy 18: 9-13) As R.C. Sproul put it in his book *The Prayer of the Lord*:

> *I think the greatest weakness in the church today is that almost no one believes that God invests His power in the Bible. Everyone is looking for power in a program, in a methodology, in a technique, in anything and everything but that in which God has placed it— His Word. He alone has the power to change lives for eternity, and that power is focused on the Scriptures.*

Therefore, contrary to the popular thinking of the day which scorns exclusiveness, it is necessary to clearly say that seeking life-changing spiritual exercise by working out with the Word of God, the Bible, is the only true method that has God's seal of approval.

Yet, the ignorance of the content of the Bible that exists among so many faithful church-going Christians today is appalling. While Martin Luther instructed people to memorize the Book of Romans, it is sad but true that many can't find the Book of Romans in their Bibles. But this is nothing new. In his book *Real*

Christianity, written in the 18th century, William Wilberforce wrote:

> Why is it so hard to get people to study the Scriptures? Common sense tells us what revelation commands: 'Faith comes by hearing, and hearing by the word of God'--'Search the Scriptures'--'Be ready to give to everyone a reason of the hope that is in you.' These are the words of the inspired writers, and these injunctions are confirmed by praising those who obey the admonition. And yet, for all that we have the Bible in our houses, we are ignorant of its contents. No wonder that so many Christians know so little about what Christ actually taught; no wonder that they are so mistaken about the faith that they profess."

You Need To "Work Out with God's Word"

But, there are many Christians who love the Word of God and use it faithfully, and their lives reflect the results. They realize that they will never exhaust the benefits received from God's Word. They know that there is always more to learn about the all-important subjects of God's grace, mercy, and forgiveness.

I have known Christians who desire to search the Scriptures because they are motivated by the

14

goodness and love of God. They have, as the psalmist declared, "tasted and seen that the Lord is good." (Psalm 34: 8) They faithfully hear the Word of God every Sunday. When Bible classes are offered, they seem to always be present.

But not everyone faithfully comes to the Word of God because they have tasted of God's goodness and want more. There are other Christians, and I believe they are in the majority, who will not pursue any life changing spiritual exercise until they are motivated by personal need. If they are not satisfied with themselves, if they are passing through trials and adversities, they will seek God to change their lives or grant them his peace and joy.

Being motivated by personal need and dissatisfaction is not only effective when dealing with spiritual exercise. It is also a powerful motivation to get us to physically exercise as well.

Motivated by Dissatisfaction

Many years ago, I stepped out of the shower, looked at myself in the mirror and said, "uk!" I was so overweight. Having been an athlete in my younger days, I was not happy with my appearance. I was badly out of shape. In addition, my extra weight and protruding "gut" was placing unnecessary strain on my legs. My knees often hurt, and my sciatic nerve repeatedly became agitated.

I decided to go on a weight loss program. I had often threatened to lose weight but could never get myself to give up the extra helping or the midnight bowl of ice cream. But this time, everything was there waiting for me. My daughter had gone on a weight loss program and left the supply of fast slimming "shakes" and soups on the kitchen counter. So, on the spur of the moment one morning, I decided to give it a try. I drank my first "filling shake" and really enjoyed it. Thus, I ate less food that day. After a few days on the program, I began to see some results. My weight was decreasing. I started doing sit-ups, which before had been nearly impossible since I had difficulty bending my middle.

After about two months, I had lost over 20 pounds. My size 40 pants were falling down. My suit jackets felt like burlap sacks. I went down the basement and searched through the wardrobe in which I had kept all my old pants and jackets which had gradually become too small for me. I discovered that they fit again. And boy, did I feel good!

The problem is, as the years went by, I "fell off the wagon," so to speak, and put the weight back on.

Over the years, I have gone through three or four weight loss efforts. Therefore, diligence is necessary. You can never say, "There, I did it," and believe that the struggle is over. For this reason, it is suggested that even after you reach your desired weight, you should continue to step on the scale.

The same is true with the Christian life. I have known many who have had some life-changing Christian experience, discovered some immediate changes in their actions and attitudes, and believed that their struggle was over only to discover that within a brief time, their problems returned. They couldn't figure out what happened.

Therefore, "working out with the Word of God" must be a daily practice. We need to daily "step on the scale" and assess our spiritual condition and repent of our sins. Our sinful nature remains until the day we bury "old Adam" in the dust from whence he came.

Changes in habits or lifestyle are often motivated by personal dissatisfaction. Those who become dissatisfied or disgusted with themselves might finally decide to do something about it. The alcoholic who almost kills himself and possibly other innocent people in an automobile accident will be forced to seek help. The husband and wife who discover that their children are being emotionally injured by their constant arguing and fighting might finally decide to seek counseling. Those who put off going to the dentist are forced into it by a toothache.

Of course, for personal dissatisfaction to prompt change, there must be a way of changing the condition that is causing the dissatisfaction. There must be a better way to live. If I would have become dissatisfied with my height, rather than my weight, I would have been out of luck. While doing something about my weight is possible, I am stuck with my height.

There are things in life we are stuck with, but other things can be changed. There is a great deal of wisdom involved in knowing the difference.

Unhappy with Your Inner Life

I don't think there are many people in our world who would say they are truly satisfied with themselves. While they may not be disturbed by their physical condition or external appearance, they are not pleased with their "Inner life," their emotions, attitudes, or personality. We all desire to be different. This is evidenced by the great popularity today of self-help books. We look at other people and wish we had some of their characteristics or traits. Of course, we might be surprised to learn that other people might be looking at us and feeling the same way.

If you go to church and hear the Word of God or are familiar with the teachings of the Bible, you know that love, joy, peace, hope, contentment, and patience are important traits in a Christian's life. Jesus promised, "I have come that you might have an abundant life." (John 10: 10) He promised to his disciples that they would have peace and joy. Yet, you might look at yourself and find very few of those abundant life traits manifested in your life. During your circumstances of life, you might be wondering, "where is that joy and peace?"

By the way of comparison, let's say you lacked physical strength or stamina, and you were not suffering from any physical ailment, what would be the diagnosis? Your doctor would probably tell you that you are not getting enough exercise or eating the right foods. Perhaps you are deficient in certain vitamins and minerals. Perhaps you need some iron in your system. to get to the cause of your spiritually run-down condition, ask yourself the obvious questions:

"Am I exercising myself spiritually? Am I receiving sufficient spiritual nourishment?" You cannot expect to sit in church and be spiritually nourished one hour

19

per week, be influenced and motivated by the world the rest of the week and expect to experience the joy and peace Jesus promised. Your diet and your exercise are not properly balanced.

In a Bible Class one Sunday I asked the question: "How many of you wish that you had more joy and peace and that you were more loving, kinder, gentler people?" Every hand went up. I was not surprised. I asked further, "How many of you believe that it is the will of God for you to be more loving and to have more joy and peace?" Again, every hand went up. I asked one more question: "How many of you believe that if you spend more time reading and studying the Bible that it will make a difference and produce more of those qualities'?" Again, the response was unanimous.

It is God's will for you to grow and to change, and he has provided you with the means to do it. The Apostle Peter writes: "Like newborn babies, crave pure spiritual milk, so that by it you may grow up in your salvation (I Peter 2: 2)." The "pure spiritual milk" is the Word of God, the Bible. God desires for you to "crave" his Word and thereby spiritually grow. The Bible tells you to "exercise yourself in godliness."

There are many spiritual ingredients in addition to love, joy, peace, hope and contentment that are, according to the Bible, a part of the Christian life. For example, the writer to the Hebrews prays that "the God of peace... equip you with everything good to do his will, and may he work in you what is pleasing to him." (Hebrews 13: 21) In his letter to Timothy, the Apostle Paul encourages Timothy to use the Word of God so that he would be "thoroughly equipped and lacking nothing." (2 Timothy 3: 17) Whatever your personal need, God's Word does have a solution. God has made specific promises concerning you and your situation of life.

Sword of the Spirit

In Ephesians 6:10-17 The Apostle Paul lists the armor of God. In verse 17 he instructs us to "take the sword of the Spirit which is the Word of God."

The devil does not tempt us to sin. That might sound strange, but have you ever noticed the absence of the devil in the Old Testament? After tempting Adam and Eve to disobey God he disappears from the scene. Why? After Adam and Eve fell into sin their nature was corrupted. They became sinners by nature and no longer required the devil to tempt them to sin. They could do it very much on their own without his assistance.

Now, the temptation of the devil is focused upon what we believe and confess to be true. If you decide to "work out with the Word of God" you will experience temptation. You will come to believe and confess the wonderful truths of the promises of the Gospel. As he said to Adam and Eve, he will now say to you, "Did God really say?" In such times of temptation, when our faith is being called into question, we use the Word of God as the "sword of the Spirit" and confront the devil with what God has said to be true. In Matthew 4, Jesus was tempted by the devil. On each occasion, he confronts the devil with the Word of God, and the devil finally gave up

Many church goers today do not experience temptation because they really don't believe anything. When asked if their sins were forgiven and they were going to heaven, they reply, "I sure hope so." Such a person is no threat to the devil and will be left alone in unbelief.

If the Word Works, What's the Hang-up?

I believe most Christians would agree that if they read and studied the Bible more and thereby "spiritually exercised," they would be positively affected. Would you agree? If so, why doesn't it happen? Why don't more Christians faithfully work out with God's Word? Having been a pastor for more than 50 years, I have made the following observations:

First, I believe many have difficulty getting any benefit out of reading or studying the Word of God, because they claim that they are not able to understand it. They have the wrong impression that studying the Bible is reserved for pastors, Bible students and theologians. They think that pastors go to seminary to study the Bible in the same way doctors go to medical school to study their medical texts and lawyers study their volumes of legal precedent.

For example, many years ago, I decided to telephone most of the faithful members of my congregation and invite them to come to Sunday morning Bible Class. One man responded to my request by saying, "No, Bible class is not for me. Thank you for inviting me, Pastor, but I really don't understand the Bible. It's your job to understand the Bible. I'll come to church every Sunday and listen to your sermons, but please don't ask me to come to Bible class."

While the Bible appears to be difficult to understand, this is not the case. There are many things that appear difficult to comprehend until you learn how they work. Remember your first encounter with a computer program? Would God offer promises to this world in a book that only a select few could understand? This would not be reasonable.

23

Think about it. The Apostle Paul wrote his epistles to people whom we would regard as primitive. He essentially says the same in 1 Corinthians when he wrote: "Brothers, think of what you were when you were called. Not many of you were wise by human standards; not many were influential; not many were of noble birth (1:26)." Would the Apostle write letter to Christians that they were unable to comprehend? This would be foolishness.

The problem is not the difficulty of the Bible, but rather the fact that most Christians don't know how to use the Bible. No one has ever taught them the simple principles and techniques needed to work out with the Word of God. In the same way, it is necessary to learn the techniques for working out with exercise equipment for physical conditioning by reading the instructions, it is also necessary to learn how to work out with the equipment that God has given for our spiritual growth.

Secondly, I believe there are Christians who are not happy with themselves but shy away from spiritual exercise because they are afraid of getting too religious and having to make some external changes in their lifestyles. They fear that if they get too spiritual they will no longer be able to enjoy a glass of beer or puff away on their favorite cigar. Perhaps they think they must spend more time in church and give up their bowling or golf. Perhaps they don't want to become like some of the Bible-toting, "goody-two-shoes" committed, born-again Christians they have met who boast of what they were and what they have become. Perhaps they are not very happy with themselves but feel that the "religious solution" is worse than their problems. So, they seek to live with themselves despite their dissatisfaction.

I want to assure you that, like embracing a physical fitness program, once you undertake a spiritual fitness program and see the positive results, you will be thrilled. There is nothing to fear. The Holy Spirit is not interested in turning you into a "spiritual prude." He simply wants you to have an abundant life and be equipped to deal with adversity. I have never met anyone who chose to begin working out with the Word of God and later regretted it.

Thirdly, by nature we are all spiritually lazy. In the same way, we may put off embracing a new diet or exercise program even though we are dissatisfied with our physical condition, the same is true of our spiritual condition. We might be dissatisfied with our inner life, but we don't want to make the decision to do anything about it.

In his book *Knowing Scripture*, R.C. Sproul writes

Here, then, is the real problem of our negligence. We fail in our duty to study God's Word not so much because it is difficult to understand, not so much because it is dull and boring, but because it is work. Our problem is not a lack of intelligence or a lack of passion. Our problem is that we are lazy.

This is a serious matter. while being in good physical condition is good and God-pleasing, God takes far more seriously our spiritual condition. The Bible tells us to "pursue" spiritual growth resulting in change. In the Book of Revelation, our Lord Jesus addresses and warns the various churches of that day. One of those churches, the Church at Laodicea, was guilty of spiritual contentment. Jesus describes their "lack of spiritual growth" as being lukewarmness. He says, "So because you are lukewarm - neither hot nor cold - I am about to spit you out of my mouth." (Revelation 3: 16)

If you feel that you are spiritually lazy and often lukewarm, it is time to repent and spring into action and do something about it. Don't put it off any longer. But, and this is very important, know what to expect from God's Word.

God Tells You the Truth

When you enter a physical exercise program you must be realistic. In my case, for example, it might be possible for me to lose some weight and tone up my muscles, but if I think that I am going to recapture my youth and get my body to do some of the things it could do thirty years ago, I will be sorely disappointed and frustrated.

God will not give you unrealistic expectations for your workout with his Word. He will tell you exactly what you can expect from this sinful world and what you, as one of his children, can expect him to do for you. Jesus told his disciples: "I have told you these things so that in me you may have peace. In this world, you will have trouble. But take heart! I have overcome the world." (John 16: 33)

Jesus makes it clear. In the world, you will have trouble, but in your relationship with him, you will have peace, because he overcame the world. Jesus was a realist!

There are many Christians who hold unrealistic expectations of what God has promised to them. Thus, they become disillusioned. For example, some make the mistake of thinking that when they exercise themselves spiritually by claiming and confessing what they believe are divine promises, it will make a difference in the circumstances of their life. They equate spiritual growth with having their circumstances changed or gaining prosperity or success so that life treats them better.

If you embark on a spiritual fitness program with such goals, you will be badly disappointed. In the words of the popular song of the past, God "did not promise you a rose garden." But he did promise grace to help in time of need. Exercising yourself spiritually will change the way you deal with the circumstances of life. Thus, you will no longer live under the circumstances, but you will be enabled to overcome the circumstances.

My oldest son played football in high school and college. He carried the ball and therefore became the target of the tacklers. Many times, I saw him get tackled very hard, knocked over and pushed back. But when the pile of bodies got untangled, much to my relief, he got up again and walked back to the huddle.

The reason he could get up again was because he was in good physical condition. He lifted weights. His muscles were built up. He had stamina.

It would be totally unrealistic for me to say that as a Christian you will never get "tackled" by the devil, the world, or your own sinful nature. At times, you will get knocked over and have your face pushed in the mud of adversity. Working out with the Word of God will not keep you from getting knocked over or pulled down by situations of life, but it will enable you to stand up again! It will enable you to use the "sword of the Spirit" against the wiles of the devil.

God wants to change you so that you can stand up again when the adversities of life knock you down. These changes take place as the result of working out spiritually with his Word.

Changing Your Heart and Renewing Your Mind

I am sure that you have heard people say, "My life has been changed!" What does that mean? It undoubtedly means more than adjustments in physical weight or appearance. It would go beyond changes in habits or external behavior. While external or physical changes might cause a change in a person's life or even be the result of a change in the person's life, life itself is more than the physical, more than the external. The person who says, "my life has been changed," is dealing with internal matters.

29

We are living in a self-help age. If you search through the psychology section in your local secular bookstore, you will discover a veritable plethora of how-to-change-your-life books.

Jesus made it very clear in his teachings that we all have "heart problems." He said, "out of the heart flow evil thoughts, murders, adulteries, etc." (Matthew 15: 19) While medical science can transplant hearts, only the Word of God is able to change hearts. Of course, Jesus and medical science are not talking about the same thing. While medical science refers to the physical blood pump, Jesus is talking about the "inner man," or the real "you," living within your physical body.

In his Sermon on the Mount (Matthew 5-7), Jesus made it clear that immoral human behavior was prompted by inner heart problems. Much to the dismay of those who boasted of their outer life and external behavior, Jesus said that lust and adultery are one and the same things as are hatred and murder, coveting and stealing. The Bible makes it very clear that God works in his people "inside-out." He wants to change our hearts. And for this purpose, he uses his Word.

In the New Testament, there is a wealth of material which describes the condition of the human heart. For example, where our treasure is, our heart will be. (Matt. 6: 21) Our mouth will speak what is in our heart. (Matt. 12: 34) We forgive others from the heart. (Matt. 18: 35) We love the Lord with our heart. (Matt. 25: 37) Mary pondered the birth of Jesus her heart. (Luke 2: 19) The heart can be opened or closed to God's Word. The heart can be enlightened. Our hearts can condemn us. We believe with our hearts. The apostle Paul tells us that the peace of God will keep our hearts and minds in Christ Jesus. (Phil. 4: 7) Working out with the Word of God will change your heart.

The Bible also teaches that the condition of your mind is very important. In fact, the Apostle Paul says that your life will be transformed because of the renewing of your mind. (Romans 12: 2) How does this work?

Your mind functions very much the same way as a computer. A computer is only as good and effective as the program you load into it. If the program doesn't work, no matter how big or fast the computer is, it is useless. There is a computer principle which states "garbage in equals garbage out." What you put into the computer will determine what you get out of it.

While your mind is far more powerful than any computer, the "garbage in/garbage out" principle is the same. We have all been programmed by the devil, the world, and our own sinful nature to respond in a certain way to the events and circumstances of life. The manner in which you respond to life determines your level of joy, peace, hope and contentment.

The Bible says to set your minds on the things of the Spirit (Romans 8: 5) and to think about those things that are honorable, good, and praiseworthy. (Phil. 4: 8)

Working out with the Word of God will have a positive effect upon your mind. It will change what you believe about life. You will reject error and embrace truth. Jesus said: "You will know the truth, and the truth will set free." (John 8: 32)

While entering a physical exercise program will affect your muscles and increase your physical stamina, working out with the Word of God will change your heart and renew your mind. As a result, the way you deal with the adversities of life will be changed. The Apostle Paul was an expert in spiritual exercise. He wrote: "I have learned to be content whatever the circumstances... I have learned the secret of being content in any and every situation." (Phil.4: 10,12) Such results are specifically promised by God in his Word. You can realistically embrace these expectations and not be disappointed.

The Word of God Creates Faith

There is a popular notion that everyone must believe in something. A baseball pitcher some years ago, led the cheers for his team by saying, "You gotta believe!" Years ago, singer Tony Bennett popularized the notion of believing when he sang, "I believe for every drop of rain that falls, a flower grows."

If everyone believes in something, what do they believe in? Where do people place their faith? Some believe in the American system. Many place their faith in themselves. Others trust in the benefits of hard work and responsible living, or the "golden rule." Some would say that it makes no difference what you believe, if you are sincere. Of course, a great many claim to believe in God. Our coins echo the sentiment, "In God we trust."

What does it mean to believe in God?

Faith, trust, or belief in God is directly joined to the promises of God. You will discover in your workout with the Word that God has made promises and offers many spiritual benefits. Your response to those many benefits is defined as faith. Where you have faith, you must have promise. Where you have promise, there faith operates. Faith is the instrument whereby you receive the promises of God and enjoy the benefits.

There are Christians today who believe God for health, wealth, success and prosperity even though no such promises exist in the Bible. To claim a blessing from God that God has not promised is not faith, but presumption. It would be utter foolishness to trust God to give you the winning Powerball numbers. Where does the Bible say that God wants you to be a multi-millionaire?

Faith is a vital ingredient! The Bible says that without faith it is impossible to please God.

The magnificent quality of the Word of God is such that it will produce in you the faith that you need to receive the spiritual benefits the Word offers. The manner God devised to work in you through his Word is amazing. It would be like a diet or exercise program offering, in addition to weight loss and muscle toning, the will-power needed to stay with the program. That would be one amazing diet or exercise program!

In the Word of God, you are not only offered many promises and spiritual benefits, but you are also given the faith to believe and receive these promises and benefits. Therefore, when you work out with the Word of God, you should expect that your faith will grow. The Holy Spirit will produce faith so that you trust the promises of God and cling to them.

Think of it in this way...

When Jesus died on the cross and rose again, God granted to us many, many benefits. In a sense, we can speak of these benefits as spiritual wealth deposited by God in a checking account with our names on it. When we became Christians, we were given our check books. God also provided us with the Bible which tells us what is available in that account. In this analogy, *the function of faith is to write checks and draw off the account.*

Of course, if a person lives and dies and never writes a check, he never appropriates any of the benefits. What a tragedy! He was a spiritual millionaire and lived and died a spiritual pauper! Working out with the Word of God uncovers many treasures of God's grace and mercy.

Unclaimed Wealth

The Gospel of Jesus Christ promises and offers to us the forgiveness of our sins, peace, joy, contentment, and eternal life in heaven. The failure to understand and believe these promises causes us to lose out on the promised benefits. This is very serious. Our eternal life is at stake.

As a parish pastor, I can recall many sad incidents in which faithful church members missed the benefits of the death and resurrection of Jesus Christ because they did not know what God had promised. They were still in the dark. Their eyes were closed to what God had done for them. Thus, they were suffering, plagued by their sin and guilt. The prophet Hosea, referring to the people of his day, declared: "My people are destroyed from a lack of knowledge." (4: 6)

I was visiting one afternoon with an elderly gentleman. He was about 85 years old and growing weaker each day. He knew that he was going to die soon. He was a man who had been a member of a Christian congregation all his life. He had served on various boards and committees and faithfully supported the work of the church.

After we prayed together, he said to me, "Pastor, I'm scared to die. I do not know whether I am going to heaven. I don't know if I have done enough to get to heaven. I have so many doubts."

After going to church for so many years, somehow, he did not know that eternal life was a gift of God. Even though God had provided for his eternal life through the death and resurrection of the Lord Jesus, he was still trying to work his way into heaven. As a result, he was suffering from fear and uncertainty. I shared with him the bad news that he most certainly had not done enough to go the heaven, and the Good News that a major benefit of the death of Jesus Christ on the cross and His glorious resurrection was that eternal life in heaven was not something to be earned, but a gift from God.

Would it not be a tragedy if this man, a church member all his life, had missed the benefit of eternal life in heaven? Of course, it is impossible to make such a judgment because we are not able to examine the heart to determine whether faith is present. But, the man's confession of fear and doubt was a cause for deep concern. Based on his own confession, his eternal salvation was in jeopardy. The issue had not been settled.

A Matter of Life or Death?

A friend with whom I regularly played golf recently entered the hospital for open heart by-pass surgery. Numerous arteries were clogged. After going through the surgery, the doctor put him on a strict diet and exercise program. For him, the physical conditioning program was not a nice means for getting in shape or becoming a more effective golfer, *it is a matter of life or death.*

Spiritual conditioning, or working out with God's Word and promises, may for some of you also be a matter of eternal life or death.

Part 2: Preparing to Workout

Before beginning any workout session or engaging in any form of physical exercise, preparation is necessary. If you are running, jogging, playing basketball or tennis, you should begin by stretching out the muscles, particularly the hamstring. Baseball and football players, before playing the game, engage in calisthenics to get the body working and the muscles ready to perform. The same is true with undertaking a workout session with the Word of God.

A Unique Book

The Bible is a unique book. The writers were inspired by the Holy Spirit. The Apostle Peter writes: "Above all, you must understand that no prophecy of Scripture came about by the prophet's own interpretation. For prophecy never had its origin in the will of man, but men spoke from God as they were carried along by the Holy Spirit (2 Peter 1.20-21)."

The words of the Bible are God's powerful words which cause results to take place in the lives of people. The Bible is a supernatural book. It produces supernatural results. When God created the heavens and the earth, he merely spoke the words. When our Lord Jesus healed people of their afflictions, he merely spoke the words. God works through words.

The words of the Bible are God's powerful supernatural words.

The apostle Paul describes the words of the Gospel of Jesus Christ as being "the power of God" (Romans 1:16). The Greek word which is translated power is *dunamis*, from which we derive the English word "dynamite." We might say that the words of the Bible are "dynamite," words which release the very power of God. For this to take place, the Holy Spirit had to inspire the human writers.

The Bible does not merely communicate human thoughts, memories, and instructions. If you want to understand the words and promises of God, you cannot read the Bible in the same way you would read a novel or a history text. While the words of the Bible in and of themselves are not difficult, they are words that were written under the direct influence of the Holy Spirit. God himself communicates to us through the words of the Bible. The Holy Spirit inspired the very words and thoughts that were recorded by these sacred writers.

Bible Stories

Of course, there are many sections in the Bible, such as stories of Old Testament heroes and heroines or incidents in the life of Jesus, that might be read like a short story. Such stories offer interesting and important reading. Many of you are probably already familiar with a good number of Bible stories. Through these narratives, we gain insight into our relationship with God. Even though Bible stories may be easy reading, the Holy Spirit still works through them, seeking to draw an application to our own lives.

Bible stories are especially effective in teaching children. Perhaps you recall learning Bible stories from your Sunday school days and taking home your leaflet with the full-color picture on the cover depicting the heroic acts of Moses, Joshua, or David. In my mind, I can still see the picture of Daniel praying in the lion's den.

But while Bible stories are valuable because they teach us about our relationship with God, the real solid food or meat is found in the teaching sections of the Bible, especially in the New Testament epistles such as Romans. Here we encounter the all-important application of the death and resurrection of the Lord Jesus Christ to our lives. We discover the mystery of the Gospel.

If we think of Bible stories as the milk of the Word because they are easy to read and digest, the New Testament epistles, such as Paul's letter to the Romans, are the meat of the Word. They are meat because we must chew on them. They cannot be immediately swallowed and digested.

Inspiration and Enlightenment

Natural knowledge, reason, and intelligence, while being valuable gifts from God, will not comprehend the Holy Spirit's supernatural truth. While our natural intelligence may help us to study the biblical words, read Bible stories and understand the social and historical context in which they were written, only the Holy Spirit can communicate to us the benefits contained in God's powerful words and thereby change our lives.

Martin Luther wrote: "All men have a darkened heart, so even if they know how to tell and present all that Scripture contains, yet they are unable to feel and truly know it."

Inspiration of the writer demands the enlightenment of the reader. This is a very important truth. If, for example, an author writes in English, you must be able to read English to understand him. If the words are written in Greek, you must be able to read Greek. If the author writes using a certain code, you must be familiar with the code. But if the author writes under the direct influence and inspiration of the Holy Spirit, you must be influenced and enlightened by the same Holy Spirit to understand the meaning of the words and receive the benefits they offer.

Think of it in this way: A radio station transmits words and sounds into the air. Some of the words are AM words while others are FM words. This defines the way the words or sounds are modulated or regulated as they are transmitted. Some are regulated by their amplitude or size. This is called AM. Others are regulated by their frequency. This is called FM. To receive these words and hear them, you must have a 'receiver." Some receivers will accept FM words and others will accept AM words. If you have an AM radio you cannot receive FM sounds. They are not compatible.

In the same way, the Bible speaks of two dimensions in this world. There is a "natural" dimension and a "spiritual" dimension. The natural dimension relates to basic human life. The biblical Greek word that is translated 'natural" is *psychikos* or pertaining to the human mind. From this word we get "psychology," which is a study of the natural human mind. The truths of history or science or mathematics are natural truths. They are grasped by the natural capabilities of the human mind.

The words of the Bible are not a part of that natural dimension but are a part of the spiritual dimension. While there is of course a natural dimension to the Bible in that it deals with facts of history and is written in human language, for spiritual knowledge and understanding to be gained and spiritual benefits to be received from the Bible, the mind of the reader must be enlightened, or illuminated, by the Holy Spirit. Without his gracious enlightenment, we are doomed to say, "I don't understand the Bible."

If the Holy Spirit inspired the writers to write, He must therefore enlighten the readers so that they understand what is written. The Holy Spirit's inspiration of the writer requires the Holy Spirit's enlightenment of the reader.

In his *Institutes of the Christian Religion*, John Calvin defined enlightenment as taking place "when the Spirit, with a wondrous and special energy, forms the ear to hear and the mind to understand." He also wrote that "whatever is not illuminated by his Spirit is wholly darkness."

In Ephesians 1:17-18, the Apostle Paul wrote: "I keep asking that the God of our Lord Jesus Christ, the glorious Father, may give you the Spirit of wisdom and revelation, so that you may know him better. I pray also that the eyes of your heart may be enlightened in order that you may know the hope to which he has called you, the riches of his glorious inheritance in the saints."

What is Enlightenment?

The human mind is a strange and mysterious thing. It has tremendous capabilities. It can know, understand, feel, think, reason, determine, remember, invent, and discover. Great minds can grasp incredible concepts and solving complicated problems. Yet for less trained minds, certain concepts are beyond their limits. I remember trying to explain the workings of a computer to my 85-year-old father. He interrupted my explanation by saying, "Donald, forget it. It's beyond me!"

There are times when the mind is "enlightened," or a person has what psychologists call an "aha experience." Something finally clicks, and what previously had been cloudy, and obscure is now clear and able to be understood.

According to the dictionary, to enlighten means "to give to the mind revealing or broadening knowledge," or "to give the light of truth." Enlightenment is the illumination of the mind by which the "eyes of the understanding" are opened. Thus, a problem finds a solution. A puzzling concept is finally understood. A good idea begins to emerge. Cartoonists usually depict enlightenment by drawing the picture of an illumined light bulb over the head of a character.

When I was a freshman in high school I had the hardest time understanding the "factoring" of algebraic equations. The concept just didn't register with me. I still remember the evening while doing my algebra homework that I received a flash of insight. My mind sorted out all the information, and suddenly everything fit together, and the concepts became clear. After "being enlightened," I could "factor" anything no matter how many "x's" or "y's" were in the equation. The light bulb went on! My mind was illumined or "enlightened."

Simple psychological enlightenment causes your eyes to look at something in a new and different way. You are all familiar with optical illusions. Perhaps some of you have seen the inkblot picture of the face of Christ. When you look at the picture, all you see is a mass of inkblots. But suddenly, the light goes on and you clearly see the face of Christ. After being "enlightened," every time you look at the picture all you see is the face of Christ. Those who remain "in the dark" and only perceive inkblots become the objects of your instruction.

" See, here's the eyes. Here's the nose, the chin. . . don't you see it?" you explain. "Look carefully. Do you see the face of Christ?"

"No, I don't see it!"

"What's wrong with you?" you ask impatiently. "It's so clear!"

Those who are enlightened often demonstrate little patience toward those who remain "in the dark."

Jesus and His Disciples

The disciples of our Lord Jesus had the same problem in understanding the teachings of their Master. They were often confused as to his ministry and purposes, even though he clearly explained himself, using all kinds of parables and illustrations. Their minds had to be opened. Their eyes had to be enlightened.

The disciples were having difficulty receiving the words of Jesus because they were not spiritually in tune with him. Their minds did not comprehend the spiritual truths which Jesus spoke. They were not equipped to hear and receive what Jesus was talking about. Something inside them had to be adjusted before they could understand. Jesus was speaking AM words and they were equipped with FM receivers. For them to receive and understand spiritual insight and understanding, their minds had to enlightened, or illuminated. Their eyes had to be opened!

After Jesus rose from the dead, on Easter evening he caught up with two of his disciples who were heading home to Emmaus after celebrating the Passover in Jerusalem. But even though they were followers of Jesus, they did not recognize him. They were very upset by the events that had taken place in Jerusalem. Their Lord and Master had been put to death, and they were discussing these events. Jesus, who was a stranger to them, explained to them from the Old Testament that these events were necessary. It was God's intention for his Messiah to suffer and to die.

When they arrived at Emmaus, since it was evening, they invited this Stranger to spend the night with them. At the supper table Jesus broke the bread and gave it to them. At that point their eyes were opened. They saw him. They recognized him as being Jesus. He then disappeared from their sight.

In some miraculous fashion, Jesus caused the eyes, the minds, and the hearts of these disciples to become spiritual "receivers." They said to each other, "Were not our hearts burning within us while he talked with us on the road and opened the Scriptures to us?"

This same type of eye-opening experience took place with all the disciples of Jesus immediately before he ascended into heaven. Jesus gathered his disciples together and taught them from the Scriptures that it was necessary for him to suffer and die so that repentance and the forgiveness of sins would be preached to all people. In Luke 24:45 we read this simple yet startling verse: "Then he opened their minds so they could understand the Scriptures."

He opened their minds! It was a miracle! Jesus enabled his disciples to understand, and it produced great results.

Praying for the Holy Spirit

How do we receive the enlightenment of the Holy Spirit? Are their steps involved? Are there preparations that we should make before the Holy Spirit will enlighten our understanding of the divine Word?

In studying the subject of the enlightenment of the Holy Spirit, most theologians who deal with it speak of prayer as a necessary preparation for receiving enlightenment. One eighteenth-century teacher of the Bible referred to prayer as an "auxiliary" or accessory or partner to the enlightenment of the Holy Spirit. He wrote:

Just as no one can see the sun without the sun, no one can know God without God, without divine illumination. The Scriptures are not understood in a beneficial way without the Spirit by whom they were brought about; we must daily implore his grace and enlightenment by our prayers.

Praying that the Holy Spirit will open our eyes to the truth that is revealed in the Bible is a very important but often neglected practice. We should approach the Word of God with the recognition that we are dealing with God's Word. The Bible is unlike any other book. As we discussed before, the Bible is a supernatural book which cannot be grasped by mere natural reason. Martin Luther wrote:

You should completely despair of your own sense and reason, for by these you will not attain the goal ... Rather kneel down in your private little room and with sincere humility and earnestness pray God through His dear Son, graciously to grant you His Holy Spirit to enlighten and guide you and give you understanding.

In a letter written in 1518 to George Spalatin, Martin Luther's friend and advisor, Luther answers Spalatin's question regarding the method for studying Scripture. He wrote:

To begin with, it is absolutely certain that one cannot enter into the [meaning of] Scripture by study or innate intelligence. Therefore, your first task is to begin with prayer. You must ask that the Lord in his great mercy grant you a true understanding of his words, should it please him to accomplish anything through you

for his glory and not for your glory or that of
any other man. For there is no one who can teach
the divine words except he who is their author,
as he says, "They shall all be taught by God."
You must therefore completely despair of your
own diligence and intelligence and rely solely on
the infusion of the Spirit. Believe me, for I have
had experience in this matter.

Luther described those who rush into the study of the Bible without first engaging in prayer as "pigs who rush in with dirty feet."

Even though we are Christians and the Holy Spirit dwells within us, our natural sinful human nature remains an enemy of God. Our natural minds are "darkened." The apostle Paul tells us that our sinful nature conflicts with the desires of the Spirit, and the Spirit conflicts with the desires of the sinful human nature (Galatians 5:17). While the Holy Spirit desires to enlighten our minds, our sinful human nature is opposed to the light of the Holy Spirit. So, it is the Holy Spirit himself who urges us, "Seek my light! Desire my enlightenment! Learn from me!"

Perhaps some of you are asking, "Since the Holy Spirit is intimately joined to the Bible, why is it necessary for us to pray? Shouldn't the enlightenment of the Spirit take place automatically, as we read the Bible, without our prayer?"

By urging us to pray, the Holy Spirit is turning us away from our natural understanding or, as Luther put it *despairing of our own sense and reason,* so that, in seeking his gracious enlightenment, we might gain life-affecting truth from his Word. By following the urgings of the Spirit to pray, we are put into the position to receive from the Holy Spirit.

To pick up on an illustration that I used earlier, I think of prayer for the enlightenment of the Holy Spirit as switching the radio dial from AM to FM. It places us into a different mode, so to speak, so that we are tuned in to the Holy Spirit's frequency.

There are many times when it is necessary for us to switch modes. For example, to arrive home after a harried day at the office, fighting traffic all the way, or to finally finish the dishes and get the kids to bed, and to then sit down and pick up your Bible and immediately expect to be spiritually fed by the Holy Spirit is not feasible. The influences of the devil, the world, and our own sinful nature put us out of touch with the Holy Spirit. We all too easily get caught up in the things of this world or turn our attention upon ourselves. So, the Holy Spirit prompts us to switch gears, to turn our hearts and minds toward God so that we might become ready receivers of his grace.

Worship will produce the same effect, especially if we sing hymns of praise that contain good scriptural content.

The important thing to keep in mind is that our prayer or praise does not cause the Holy Spirit to come and enlighten our understanding of the Word of God. The Holy Spirit is always present where the Word of God is found. Prayer or praise changes our hearts and directs our minds unto God so that we might receive from him.

I Forgot to Pray

Because of our old sinful nature, our willingness to obey the promptings of the Spirit to pray, to worship and praise, and to seek and desire our God is often quite feeble. By nature, we are proud people and do not want to express our dependency upon God. So, we need to be continually reminded.

Just about every Saturday evening I have the same experience. Through the course of the week I do some reading and studying in preparation for my Sunday morning sermon, but putting the thoughts together is reserved for Saturday night.

So, seated on the sofa in my study, I begin to think about the text, the theme for the day, and try to come up with some good ideas that I can preach. Very often there is a struggle involved; nothing seems to fit together. Finally, the thought hits me, "You haven't prayed for enlightenment."

My first reaction to the thought is embarrassment. Why have I forgotten to pray? Why does this same failure happen week after week? So, I repent or change my mind about my natural ability to comprehend the Bible. I confess: "Lord, I am so slow to learn. Forgive me! Why is it, Lord, that I think I can understand your Word without your Holy Spirit? Open my eyes. Open my mind. Give me some good insights into your Word that I might share with your people so that they too will understand your Word and grow in their faith."

Though on the surface opening the Bible and determining to pray for enlightenment or to turn our hearts and minds toward God through praise seems rather simple, if not even mechanical, this is certainly not true. The devil, working with our natural human reason, wants us to rush into the Scriptures. Martin Luther spoke of that as coming to the Word of God as "pigs with dirty feet." The Holy Spirit himself must continually remind us and teach us to depend upon him.

The results of praying for the enlightenment of the Holy Spirit are not immediate, which might leave the impression that such prayer is ineffective. But this is not the case at all. We patiently wait upon the Holy Spirit to quicken his Word. We might compare praying for the enlightenment of the Holy Spirit to turning up the thermostat on a cold day. The results are not instantaneous, but fifteen minutes later the room is warmer.

In sermon preparation, after praying for enlightenment and expressing my dependency upon the Holy Spirit, I soon begin to receive some new thoughts regarding my sermon text and the application. This experience with the Bible is not only reserved for preachers. Every Christian who opens the Bible to a meaningful text and expresses the desire to be enlightened by the Holy Spirit will experience this same dynamic of receiving enlightened thoughts and insights into the Word of God.

In approaching the Bible, I have found that brief, spontaneous prayers for enlightenment and expressions of praise and dependency upon God are the most effective. This is not a formal prayer—a kneel-down, fold-your-hands, bow-your-head prayer—but just a simple expression of the heart toward God. It is a conscious profession of dependency upon him: "Open my eyes, Lord! Holy Spirit, enlighten my understanding! I thank you for your Word. Feed me through it."

While there is great value in developing a disciplined prayer life by setting aside time each day to pray, very often in our daily activities the brief, spontaneous expressions of the heart are the most effective forms of prayer. Martin Luther wrote that a prayer must "come from the heart spontaneously, without any prepared or prescribed words. It must speak its own language per the fervor of the heart."

Before we can see wonderful things in the Word of God, we need to pray that the Holy Spirit will open our eyes and enlighten our minds. We do not pray to "bring the Spirit." It is the Holy Spirit himself who is urging us to direct our hearts and minds toward God.

Part 3: Meditating Upon the Word of God

A good physical exercise session demands time. If you are lifting weights or working out on an exercise machine, some of the most effective exercises are the ones done slowly. It's the last muscle-straining lift or the final difficult sit-up in the series which are the most effective. If you are serious about physical exercise, you don't simply race through the session. You must sweat. You must work at it.

A spiritual exercise program is no different. When you work out with the Word of God, you simply cannot sit down, race through a chapter or two of the Bible and say, "There, I've done my workout." You may have read two chapters of the Bible, but you certainly did not get a great deal out of it.

When you take into consideration the nature of the Word of God and what you are trying to accomplish, your workout with the Word will produce beneficial results only if you take the time to ponder God's Word and meditate upon his many promises. This is not hard to understand.

Secondly, you want the Word of God to get into your heart and renew your mind. You are not looking for the mere superficial information you might receive by reading a newspaper or magazine. The content of

God's words and promises must "get into you," so to speak, to make a difference. The Bible speaks of the solid food or "meat" of the Word of God. (Hebrews 5:12-14) Meat must be chewed awhile to be digested.

Therefore, one of the necessary techniques to learn to work out with the Word of God is meditation. By this I mean to reflect upon, think about, or ponder the content of a section of Scripture, or perhaps one or two verses.

How does a Christian Meditate?

The word meditation has different, sometimes confusing meanings. Transcendental Meditation or TM, as it is called, involves the emptying of the mind of all thoughts and repeating a "mantra," which is a Hindu prayer or invocation in the Sanskrit language. The person repeating the mantra repeatedly has no idea what he is saying. Buddhism and some forms of mysticism also promote an empty-headed form of meditation.

Empty-headed meditation can be a very dangerous practice. It is an open invitation for demonic spirits to influence the mind. Most occult practices such as seeking to contact the dead or inviting the presence of an inner spirit guide begin by emptying the mind of all thoughts. These practices are strictly forbidden in the Word of God.

In contrast, when Christians meditate upon the Word of God, this does not involve maintaining a blank mind. Rather it means filling the mind with the Word of God.

For the Holy Spirit to effectively open your eyes, strengthen your faith and affect your heart and mind, you must prayerfully focus your conscious, undivided attention upon the words you are reading or studying. Working out with the Word of God means taking the time to think about the Word and promises of God. This is what it means to meditate. We give the Holy Spirit time to work with us.

Personalize the Promises

My youngest son Dan played football and ran track in high school. To get into good physical condition, he joined a local gym which offered the use of a variety of workout equipment. The director of the gym sat down with him and asked him what he wanted to accomplish in working out. Dan told him that he wanted to strengthen his muscles for football and track. The director proceeded to personalize his workout program, designing it for his size and goals.

Many people make the mistake of regarding the words of the Bible as being written to a specific people living many years ago. This is one of the reasons they have difficulty practically applying the words of the Bible to themselves today. Even when pastors teach the Bible we often get too hung up on the conditions and special circumstances of the day in which the words were written, rather than concentrating upon the application of the Word to the hearts of people today.

While it is certainly true that understanding the conditions of the day gives us insight into the application of the Word to the people of that day, what we need to clearly understand is how the Word applies to us today.

When you work out with the Word of God, you should also personalize the content of the Word, read and apply it as if it is written just for you.

Let's use the theme verses of the Book of Romans, chapter 1: verses 16 and 17. As we consider the verses, I will ask you questions about the verses. You think about the questions and provide the answers. Read carefully the verses:

I am not ashamed of the gospel for it is the power of God for the salvation of everyone who believes; first for the Jew and then for the Gentile. For in the gospel, a righteousness from God is revealed, a righteousness that is by faith from first to last, just as it is written: "The righteous shall live by faith."

We first pray, "Lord, by your Holy Spirit, help me to understand your Word. Open my eyes that I might see. Make your Word a personal, life-changing word written specifically to me."

The verse begins, "I am not ashamed of the gospel." Of course, the "I" is the Apostle Paul, but is it not also you? Put your name in place of the "I" and boldly confess: "(Your name) is not ashamed of the gospel."

Further, take out the word "everyone" and replace it with your name. The verse would then read: "(Your name) is not ashamed of the gospel because it is the power of God for the salvation of (your name) who believes."

The Gospel is God's power! Think about that. If you want God's power at work in your life, where do you go? Where do you look? The Gospel is the power to save you. Save you from what?

You are included in the "everyone." Are you a believer? Of course, you are. Therefore, you are saved.

The Apostle says that the Gospel reveals a righteousness from God that is totally by faith. To whom does the Gospel reveal this "righteousness from God" which is by faith? Obviously, it is revealed to you. Confess that fact. "The Gospel tells me that I am righteous! Do you believe it?"

The verse ends, "The righteous shall live by faith." God has declared you righteous. Put your name in there. You live by faith! Faith in what? What is the alternative to living by faith?

Consider the well-known verse from John 3:16. "For God so loved the world that he gave his only-begotten Son, that whosoever believes in him, will not perish but have everlasting life."

There are two inclusive words in that text: world and whosoever. Personalizing the text would cause it to read like this: "For God so loved me that he gave his only-begotten Son, that since I believe in him, I will not perish, but I will have everlasting life."

Think of the simple verse from Romans 6:23: "The wages of sin is death, but the gift of God is eternal life in Christ Jesus our Lord." Consider the following personal thoughts gleaned from that verse.

The first part of the verse tells me that my sin pays a wage. What does that mean? This is a specific cause and effect reality. My sin produces death. My death will demonstrate that I am a sinner. Hmmm? That's interesting. The thought that comes to mind is this: the one fact you can declare about me at my funeral is: "He was a sinner!" Do you agree?

But God has given me the gift of eternal life in Jesus Christ. This is a gift! How do I respond to a gift? Can I earn it? Pay for it? Or do I simply receive it? Obviously, I can only receive it since it is free. Have I received the gift? Yes! Definitely! The Holy Spirit has given me faith. How do I respond? Thank you, Lord!

So, while it is true that my sin pays off the wage of death, my God gives to me a free gift of eternal life through Jesus Christ.

In your spiritual exercise, when you meditate upon the Word of God, make it your own personal word, because it is intended to be personal. It's for you! It applies to you. It speaks about your situation. By personalizing these simple verses, you not only hear a word spoken to you, but you also hear yourself confessing your faith and claiming the promises as your very own.

When you work out with the Word of God, you will discover many great "chunky" promises that God has made to you. Chew upon those promises. Personalize them. Meditate upon them. Read the verses as if the Apostle were writing his letter directly to you. Allow the Holy Spirit to speak to you through the Word.

As you read and meditate upon God's Word and the Holy Spirit opens your eyes, you will discover many changes taking place in your life. Your attitude toward life will change. Your bitterness or resentment will dissipate. Your worries and fears will be replaced with faith. Joy will be stirred within your life. You will be spiritually exercised by the living and active Word of God.

Hearing the Word

You also are in a workout session when you go to church on a Sunday morning and hear the Word of God. When you sit in church, if you want to get anything out of what is happening, you must put something into it. You cannot listen to the sermon, sing the words of the Hymns and hear the reading of the Scripture lessons as you would, for example, listen to your car radio. While your conscious thoughts may be directed elsewhere, and you are driving along, the words from the radio are simply going in one ear and out the other.

Effective listening in church demands meditating upon and pondering the words that are being spoken. If the words go in one ear and out the other, we are the ones who are losing the benefit of those words.

Hearing the Word of God means that you are consciously focused so that you meditate upon and ponder the words that are being spoken and sung. In other words, don't just sit there as a "pew-potato" who is merely fulfilling a religious duty by going to church. Be actively engaged in hearing the Word of God.

An elderly gentleman from a congregation I served as pastor was very hard-of-hearing. When our church had been built, some 60 years ago, "hearing aids" were installed in four of the pews. Well, the hearing aids eventually failed, and since the wires had been imbedded in the concrete floor, the system was nonrepairable.

This gentleman complained! Every Sunday the ushers were verbally blasted. The church secretary received two or three somewhat nasty phone calls each week. In response to his complaints, the Board of Directors purchased, at a rather sizable expense, a wireless setup for the hearing impaired, but the man never got to use it. Before the system was installed, the Lord called him home.

At his funeral I preached on the words from Romans 10:17: "Faith comes from hearing." I asked the question, "Did our brother in Christ desire to hear the Gospel of Jesus Christ?" Of course, the answer was a resounding YES! I told the story of the broken hearing aids and his response. His desire to hear the Word of God was clear evidence that the Holy Spirit was at work in his life. Based on that desire, I could declare that he believed in the Lord Jesus and was in heaven because the Gospel works!

It is especially exciting for the one preaching the Gospel to see people intently involved in hearing. I had one man in my congregation who hangs on every word that I speak. It is encouraging for me to watch his expressions of excitement and joy over the Good News of the Gospel. Every Sunday morning at the door, he has a very insightful comment to make about the content of the sermon.

By personal interaction with this man, I have come to know his deep faith. Why does he have such faith? Because he attentively hears the Word of God. If everyone in my congregation listened the way that man listened, our congregational life and ministry would be profoundly renewed. Why? Because there is spiritual life and power in God's Word.

The most important time in the Sunday morning service is when the clear message of the Gospel of Jesus Christ is being proclaimed. It is the time for you to put away all other thoughts and concerns and attentively listen, breathe a prayer for enlightenment and allow the Holy Spirit to graciously work in your mind and heart.

If you have difficulty concentrating upon the Word of God and there are empty pews in the front of the church, which there usually are, move up so that nothing will come between you and what is being proclaimed. I realize that many of you have been sitting in the same pew for years. Perhaps a change would be a good so that you might more effectively develop the practice of prayerfully and attentively listening.

Some of the most beautiful explanations of the Gospel of Jesus Christ are found in our hymns and choruses of praise. Don't look around at the other people or be self-conscious of your singing voice. Concentrate upon the words. For example, think deeply about the following hymn verse:

My hope is built on nothing less than Jesus blood and righteousness. No merit of my own I claim but wholly lean on Jesus name. On Christ, the solid rock I stand; all other ground is sinking sand.

This is a magnificent explanation of the Gospel of Jesus Christ. Much of our hymnody is rich in meaning. Think deeply about the words as you sing the hymns.

In Romans 10:17 the Apostle Paul tells us that faith is produced by hearing the "word" or "message" of Christ. Our faith does not increase as the result of having words thrown at us. It is not automatic. Faith is strengthened and increased by hearing the message. Therefore, carefully listen!

Many do not understand and cling to the message of the Gospel of Jesus Christ because they do not prayerfully and attentively listen to what is being preached. There are many distractions. The devil is continually at work to fill the mind of the hearer with other thoughts and concerns. If he cannot stop you from going to church on a Sunday morning, he will try to stop you from listening. The Word of God can be resisted by simply turning it off.

I have heard people say, "I didn't get anything out of that church service." It is because they didn't listen! They didn't put anything into it.

Facts, Not Feelings

As you work out with the Word of God, your life and experience is going to be affected. Your faith will grow. Thus, joy and peace will fill your heart. It is the effect of God's Word. The Holy Spirit guarantees such results. The Word of God will produce positive, life-changing spiritual experiences. After all, having our lives changed is the purpose of engaging in spiritual exercise.

There are different terms Christians use to define their life-changing experiences with the Lord Jesus. This results in much confusion. Some speak of a "salvation" experience. Others talk about being "born-again" or "filled with the Holy Spirit." Some say their lives were changed when they "prayed to accept Christ," or "made a decision for Jesus," or "let Jesus into their heart," or "asked Jesus to rule on the throne of their heart." Some talk about letting Jesus be "Lord of their life." I have heard people claim to have experienced "the joy of the Lord," or being filled with "the peace that passes all understanding," or having a "cleansed conscience."

The fact is, we experience God's life-changing grace as the result of the Holy Spirit opening our eyes to the truth that is found in God's Word, the Bible. There is no other way that God changes lives! No matter what you call it, the dynamic is still the same. You did not accept Christ. It was Christ who died and rose again for you. Your life was not changed because you prayed a prayer to let Jesus into your heart. The Holy Spirit changed your life when you heard the Word of truth, the Gospel of your salvation, and you believed. (Ephesians 1:13) Be sure to properly place your focus. It is very important.

For this reason, I believe that renewed involvement with the Word of God is the dynamic behind all awakenings, revivals, renewal and reformations in the Church. The Holy Spirit gives light. He opens our eyes to the Gospel of Jesus Christ and creates faith. Our lives are transformed. Thus, spiritual revival breaks out among God's people. There is no revival in the church without changed lives. There are no changed lives without the Holy Spirit. And there is no working of the Holy Spirit apart from the Word of God.

Facts, Faith and Experience

Understanding the relationship between the Word of God and personal life-changing experience is very important. For example, we previously meditated upon Romans 6:23: "The wages of sin is death, but the gift of God is eternal life in Christ Jesus our Lord." When my eyes are opened to the truth that heaven is a gift, I am filled with peace and joy. I know that I have eternal life.

If you would ask me the question: "How do you know that you are going to heaven?", I would not say, "I know because I am filled with peace and joy." I know that I am going to heaven because the Bible says that heaven is a free gift. In case I lose my assurance, peace and joy, I simply go back to the Word and promises of God regarding eternal life and the Holy Spirit does his work again.

I once asked a person the question: "How can you be sure that your sins are forgiven?"

He responded, "because my conscience is clear."

This is a wrong understanding. A clear conscience is the result of knowing that Jesus died for you. While the condition of the conscience may change, the benefits that come through the cross of Jesus Christ remain the same. Therefore, if our conscience bothers us, we go back to the cross. The Word and promises of God never change.

I heard it put this way: fact, faith, and experience were walking on top of the wall. As long as faith kept looking at the facts found in the Bible, experience always came running along behind. But as soon as faith looked back to see whether experience was coming, both faith and experience fell of the wall. Therefore, keep your eyes on the facts. Focus upon the Word of God, not on your experience.

Looking in the Wrong Place

As the result of using questionable definitions for life-changing Christian experience, the possibility of doubt arising is very real. For example, a few years ago, in my book *Christ-Esteem* I discussed the sufficiency of the person and work of Jesus Christ for life and salvation. I clearly explained that the assurance of the forgiveness of sins and eternal salvation was based upon the historical fact of the death and resurrection of Jesus Christ recorded in the Bible and not upon personal experience. We know that we are saved, forgiven, and heaven-bound, not because of our faith or experience, but because the Bible tells us that Jesus died and rose again.

One day I received a phone call from a pastor of a large congregation in the South. He had read the book and had some questions. He was a member of a denomination that taught people to answer an altar call. After identifying himself and his reason for calling, he very bluntly asked, "When were you saved?"

"When Jesus died on the cross and rose again," I answered confidently.

"What about your experience? Have you had any experience?"

"Of course, I've had experience!" I responded. "My sins are forgiven. My conscience is clear. I am a new creature in Christ, and I know that I am going to heaven."

For a few moments, there was silence. Somehow, he was stumped by my response. And then, somewhat more gently, he began to share his problem.

"Twenty-five years ago, I had a glorious salvation experience," he began. "I got saved. I was born-again. My life was totally changed. I decided to become a pastor and worked very hard at building a large congregation."

He paused and then continued with some hesitation, "Now, as a result of some personal problems, ...I am no longer sure that I have ever really been saved or born-again."

His voice reflected a deep sense of discouragement and disappointment. He continued, "what you said in your book about the certainty of salvation being based upon facts and not upon experience was very interesting."

I felt sorry for the man. I knew that it was very difficult for him to make such a confession to another pastor who was not even a part of his denomination.

I responded to him gently, yet with confidence.

"My friend, your problem is that you are looking for the certainty of your salvation in the wrong place," I explained to him. "You are looking at your experience. You didn't get saved when you went forward in response to an altar call. You were saved as a result of the death and resurrection of Jesus Christ, not as a result of your accepting Christ. Keep focused upon what God has done for you in Jesus Christ, not upon how you responded. Keep your eyes on the promises of God, not on your personal experience, be it positive or negative. Confess to yourself the truth of the Gospel of Jesus Christ. Jesus died for you. He shed his blood for you. No experience in your life can change that reality."

His response was very interesting. He said, "Why don't you Lutherans write more books?"

We continued to speak at length about the nature of Christian knowledge and certainty. I hope that I had helped him to focus his attention upon the Cross of Jesus Christ rather than upon his experience. Even though his life-changing experience of twenty-five years ago was a legitimate Christian experience, it could not be used as a basis for the certainty of forgiveness and salvation.

Back to the Bible

It is the purpose of God to call us back to his Word so that the Holy Spirit can strengthen and bolster our faith, which always needs bolstering. If we ever doubt any of the promises of God and experience fear, guilt, or worry, we should turn back to the Bible and again read and meditate upon the promises of God. Thus, the Holy Spirit will again enlighten our eyes and rekindle the certainty of God's love, grace, and forgiveness.

It is the purpose of God to call us back to his Word so that the Holy Spirit can strengthen and bolster our faith, which always needs bolstering. If we ever doubt any of the promises of God and experience fear, guilt, or worry, we should turn back to the Bible and again read and meditate upon the promises of God. Thus, the

Holy Spirit will again enlighten our eyes and rekindle the certainty of God's love, grace, and forgiveness.

For this reason, we preach the same message of Christ crucified, risen, ascended, and coming again Sunday after Sunday after Sunday. We always need to be reminded to turn our eyes upon Jesus—the Jesus of the New Testament who died for us and rose again.

Part 4: Setting Your Primary Goals

At the gym I often attend they have a host of workout apparatus. On the side of each "machine" with it's weights attached is a description of which muscles the apparatus is geared to develop. Since my primary goal has to do with tightening "the abs" I primarily use the apparatus geared for that purpose. So, when working out, defining specific goals is very important.

What Do I Need to Know?

When beginning a workout with the Word of God, the question of primary goals is very important. What do you hope to gain?

In the first line of his massive work titled *The Institutes of the Christian Religion*, John Calvin writes: "Our wisdom, in so far as it ought to be deemed true and solid wisdom, consists almost entirely of two parts: the knowledge of God and of ourselves."

We seek the enlightenment of the Holy Spirit and study the Bible to receive this twofold knowledge: the knowledge of God and of ourselves. But which should we seek first, the knowledge of God or the knowledge of ourselves?

If one were to write a formal, systematic, doctrinal treatment about God and man based upon the Bible, the teachings about God would come before the teachings about man. It would not be proper to first discuss the doctrine of man before discussing the doctrine of God. God, of course, comes first.

But if those teachings are to be applied to the human heart for creating faith and producing transformation through preaching or through writing a "workout" book of this nature, the order must be reversed. Before seeking the enlightenment of the Holy Spirit and going to the Bible so that we might discover the life-changing grace of God Christ Jesus, we must first seek to know what kind of people we are. Therefore, we first pray: "Holy Spirit, open our eyes. Enlighten us so that we might know ourselves."

Know Thyself

When we think of the word "enlightenment," positive thoughts come to mind. An enlightened person is a smarter person, or, in some ways, so to speak, a better person. He has been enlightened! He has acquired helpful knowledge and insights.

The eighteenth century is described as the "Age of Enlightenment." Through the discovery of new truths and scientific concepts, many of the archaic notions and superstitions of the Middle Ages were rejected. The world seemingly advanced. People became smarter. The quality of life improved.

With that in mind, how would you respond to this statement: "You need to have your eyes opened so that you would know what a miserable, wretched sinner you are"? Would you consider such enlightenment beneficial?

You might respond, ''No thank you. I can do very well without that kind of enlightenment."

But, what if such an eye-opening knowledge of your sin and the perversion of your human nature was a necessary prelude for pursuing an enlightened knowledge of God's life-changing love, grace, forgiveness, and power? Would you then be willing to see your sin to touch the grace of God? Would you then be willing to uncover your weakness to touch the strength of God? Would you then be willing to turn away from yourself if such a turn brought you face-to-face with the Lord Jesus Christ and his love for you?

Martin Luther wrote: "If you want to engage profitably in the study of Holy Scripture and do not want to run head-on into a Scripture closed and sealed, then learn, above all things, to understand sin aright."

David prayed, "Search me, O God, and know my heart; test me and know my anxious thoughts. See if there is any offensive way in me and lead me in the way everlasting" (Psalm 139:23,24). Because of seeing the depth of our sin, we will desire to touch the love, grace, mercy, and forgiveness of our God.

As God Sees Us

If we are willing to touch life-changing spiritual reality, we must see ourselves as God sees us: miserably weak sinners in need of grace. We will see our senseless reactions against the situations of life, our self-centeredness, our self-pity, our failure to rejoice in the Lord always, our hurt pride, our roller-coaster emotions, our desire for understanding and acceptance (rather than grace) as sins against God. As a result, we will seek God and desire the Holy Spirit to open our eyes to his truth so that we will be set free.

We need the Holy Spirit to open our eyes so that we might clearly see the degree to which sin pervades our lives to have the Holy Spirit open our eyes to the life-changing grace of God in Christ Jesus.

The Bible is very clear in revealing to us the divine estimate of human nature. Being born out of the root of Adam, we are the children of wrath (Ephesians 2:3), totally unable by nature to grasp the things of the Spirit of God (1 Corinthians 2:14). The Bible tells us that we were shaped in iniquity and born in sin (Psalm

51:5) and that the imaginations of our hearts are evil (Genesis 8:21). Within our human flesh there dwells no good thing. Even though we may desire to do good and to be good, we are unable to accomplish our lofty ideals because our nature is wrong (Romans 7:18, 19). We are in bondage to the law of sin and death (Romans 7:21-23).

The Bible says in Romans 3:23: "All have sinned and fallen short of the Glory of God." As read that verse, replace "all" with your name. YOU have sinned and fallen short of the glory. We read in Psalm 51:5: "Surely I was sinful at birth, sinful from the time my mother conceived me." While David here speaking about himself, as you read the verse apply it to you.

Putting it very simply, from God's point of view our lives are a mess! We need self-accusation, not self-esteem. We need grace, not acceptance and understanding. We need to be rescued from ourselves, not supported by a group of fellow sinners.

If you read of the experiences of other Christians who progressed in their knowledge of God's life-changing grace, you will note this combination of a deep sense of sin and failure together with a deep appreciation for God. Men the likes of Paul the apostle, John Calvin, and Martin Luther were not afraid to speak of their sinful nature and even boast of their weaknesses, because they knew of the grace of God. The writings of such men reflect a profound level of spiritual depth and insight.

Don't be afraid to confront yourself head-on and thereby uncover your sinful condition. Your pride may argue against what the Holy Spirit is trying to show you. You may struggle and squirm when he turns on the light and exposes your thoughts, attitudes, self-centeredness, priorities, and ambitions. Stripped of every pretense of righteousness, you will stand before God seeing yourself as he sees you. This is the real you, prepared to be touched by the transforming grace of God. Therefore, we pray, "Search me, O God!"

The Mysterious Gospel

The Gospel, which offers to us the forgiveness of sins, life and salvation in Jesus Christ, is the essence of Christianity. It is the instrument of the Holy Spirit. If we want to experience the life-changing power of God, we must clearly understand and receive by faith the dynamic promises of the Gospel. That message must infect our minds and be burned into our hearts. The Gospel is how God delivers to us his life-changing grace.

The Gospel, as distinguished from the Law, is always a word of promise. It tells us what God has done for us. Martin Luther defines the Gospel as a "preaching and proclamation of the grace and mercy of God through Jesus Christ, merited and won by his death."

The Gospel of Jesus Christ is a mystery. We are not able to beneficially grasp the meaning and significance of the death and resurrection of Jesus Christ through our natural reason and intelligence. The Gospel is not human wisdom; it is divine wisdom. The apostle Paul describes God's plan for reaching out to sinful mankind through the death and resurrection of his Son Jesus Christ as "secret wisdom" which can only be revealed by the Spirit (1 Corinthians 2:7-10). In fact, according to natural human reason, the wisdom of God revealed in the Gospel is foolishness. Only by the enlightenment of the Holy Spirit can we understand what God has accomplished for us in Christ Jesus.

Even though this message of the Gospel is the essence of Christianity and is revealed in the Bible, many Christians have a vague understanding of the Gospel. They may acknowledge the historical reality of the death of Jesus Christ on the cross, but often their eyes are closed as to how that message applies to them. Their hearts have not been touched and their lives affected. For this reason, they come short of experiencing God's life-changing power.

The essence of Christianity is the Gospel. While the Bible speaks about many subjects and provides many facts of history as well as many religious rules and regulations, the life-changing heart and core of the Bible is the Gospel of Jesus Christ. We read and study the Bible to learn about Jesus and hear the good news of what he has done for us.

Christian Confusion

Failure to understand the Gospel results in great confusion over the nature and teachings of Christianity. As a Christian pastor for over 50 years I have had countless opportunities to speak with people about Christianity. I have often been amazed by their gross misconceptions. It is a rare treat to find a person who truly understands what it means to be Christian.

For example, at the request of some members of my congregation I conducted a funeral for a family with whom I was not acquainted. I sat down with the niece of the deceased, who claimed to be a Christian, to get some information.

"Was your uncle a Christian?" I gently inquired.

"Of course, he was," she firmly responded. "He was a very good man. He lived a good life. Everybody liked him."

Without seeming to appear too pushy, I continued the questioning. "Well, that's great," I responded. "It's nice to know that he was such a good man, but was he a Christian?"

"He seldom went to church, if that's what you mean," she responded, becoming a little disturbed. "I think he had a Bible, but I don't know if he ever read it."

"Being a Christian," I began to explain, "is more than going to church or owning a Bible. Christians believe that their sins are forgiven and that they have eternal life because of the death and resurrection of Jesus Christ. Did your uncle believe in Jesus?"

"Oh," she replied, obviously embarrassed. "I don't know anything about that!"

This confusion is widespread. If you don't believe me, try asking some of the people with whom you work or interact daily what it means to be a Christian. See what kind of answers you get. You might be very surprised. While of course a very few would correctly define Christianity by the Gospel, others would focus on the Ten Commandments or would appeal to church membership and involvement. Still others would identify a Christian by love, or by "the Golden Rule," or by involvement in religious rites or traditions. I knew one man who identified a Christian as someone who was not a Jew. Even though we claim to be a Christian nation, only a very small percentage of alleged "Christian" people know what it means to be a Christian.

So, as you workout with the Word of God, your primary focus must be upon having your eyes opened to your sin and God's incredible grace as shows in Jesus Christ.

Part 5: Where Do You Begin?

Before applying some of the methods and techniques for working out with the Word of God, let us understand some facts about this book we call the Bible. It is not a single book but contains sixty-six little books, divided into two "testaments" or "covenants" - the "old" one and the "new" one. A testament or a covenant is an agreement between two parties. In the case of the Bible, the agreement is between God and man.

The Old Testament

The Old Testament contains thirty-nine books presenting four types of literature: law, history, prophecy, and poetry.

The first five books of the Bible (Genesis, Exodus, Leviticus, Numbers, Deuteronomy) or what is called by the Jews as the "Torah" contain the writings of Moses. The first eleven chapters of Genesis describe ancient history including the stories of Creation, the Fall into Sin, Cain and Abel, the Tower of Babel and the Flood. Beginning with Genesis 12, Moses, records the history of the children of Israel or the Jews. The primary characters are Abraham, Isaac, Jacob, Joseph and Moses. Traditionally, Abraham is dated at

2000 BC and Moses at 1500. Exodus describes the deliverance of the children of Israel from Egypt. Leviticus presents the Law of God handed down by Moses from Mount Sinai.

Because of disobedience, the Jews are forced to wander in the wilderness for forty years before entering their own land that had been promised to Abraham and his descendants – the land of Israel. In Deuteronomy (which means second law), the Law of God is again spoken to the people. The Torah ends with the death of Moses.

Most of the Old Testament records the history of the Jews or the Children of Israel. This includes the conquering and settling of the Land of Israel; the rule of the Judges; the establishment of the Monarchy; the building of the Temple in Jerusalem; the destruction of Jerusalem and the Temple by the Babylonians in 587 BC; and the return from Babylon and rebuilding of the Temple. The primary characters are Joshua, Gideon, Samson, Samuel, Saul, David, Solomon, Daniel and Ezra. The nation of Israel reached their zenith at the time of the reign of King David in about 1000 BC.

The Old Testament ends at about 350 BC. The Jews believed that God stopped inspiring writers at that time. The time from 350 BC until the birth of Jesus is called the Intertestamental Period. Various writings called the "Apocrypha" did emerge during those years which are not included in the "Protestant" Bibles but are accepted as authority by Roman Catholics.

When the Children of Israel disobeyed God, or began to follow false gods, God would raise up a prophet or "preacher" who would point out the sins of the people, speak of the judgment of God and, in most cases, offer a future hope of redemption and salvation. The main prophets were Isaiah, Jeremiah and Ezekiel. There were a host of "minor prophets." Malachi, the final prophet, is the last book in the Old Testament.

Primarily David and Solomon composed works of meditation and poetry. These are Psalms, Proverbs, Ecclesiastes and Song of Solomon. There are 150 Psalms, each one speaking of the greatness of God and offering hope and comfort to his people.

So, the Old Testament contains law, history, prophecy and poetry and was originally written in Hebrew.

The Old Testament, through the system of sacrifice where animals were sacrificed for the sins of the people and through the writings of the prophets looks forward to the coming of Messiah who would rescue his people. The Old Testament points to Jesus and is the "cradle of Christ."

It is not necessary in studying the Bible to read the entire history of Israel and the words of all the prophets – even though this is important and provides the context for the coming of Jesus, the promised Messiah. Our priority is to grow in our relationship with Jesus and this is the New Testament. Once you have firmly established your relationship with Jesus you can go back to the Old Testament and with Martin Luther "find Christ on every page."

So, for now, review the history and dates:

Genesis 1-11: Creation, Cain and Abel, Tower of Babel and Flood.

2000 - 1500 B.C: Call of Abraham, birth of Isaac, birth of Jacob and his twelve sons, including Joseph. Joseph sold into slavery in Egypt. Because of the famine in the land, Jacob and his family move to Egypt where they eventually become slaves.

1500-1000 B.C.: Moses raised up to deliver the family of Jacob that has now become a great nation. The Exodus – the giving of the Law (Ten Commandments) – wandering in the wilderness for forty years. Joshua crosses the Jordan and captures Jericho. The land ruled by Judges until the people demand a king. Saul first King of Israel, replaced by David – the greatest King.

1000 B.C.-350 B.C.: Solomon becomes King, builds the Temple in Jerusalem and the nation divides. Israel in the north and Judah in the south. Israel defeated by and taken captive by the Assyrians in 722 B.C. In 587 Nebuchadnezzar and the Babylonians defeat Judah and destroy the Temple. Persians defeat the Babylonians and King Cyrus allows the Jews to return to Jerusalem and rebuild the Temple and the walls of the city.

Here ends the Old Testament.

Between the Testaments

Before discussing the New Testament, it is important to know something of the history between the Testaments. In 587 BC, the Babylonians destroyed Jerusalem and its temple, and exported the elite members of its population to Babylon. This period is known as the Babylonian captivity. In 539 BC, the Persian defeated the Babylonians and under King Cyrus, many of the Jews returned to Jerusalem to rebuild the Temple and the walls of the city.

Now enters Alexander the Great. By 333, Alexander defeated the Persians and ruled over Israel until his death in 323. Alexander was known for spreading Greek Culture. Somewhere in the middle of the third century before Christ, the Hebrews Old Testament was translated into Greek. All the New Testament documents were written in Greek.

Between 323-167 BC, Israel was ruled first by Egypt and then by Assyria. In 167 BC, Antiochus IV "Epiphanes" a Greek king, responded to a civil war in Jerusalem by attacking the city. He outlawed the practice of the Jewish religion and desecrated the temple in Jerusalem by sacrificing a pig to the Greek god Zeus. This produced the successful revolt of the Maccabees from 167-142 BCE. The temple was re-consecrated - the basis for the Jewish celebration of Hanukah.

The Jews were independent from 167 to 63 BC. In 63 BC, the Roman general Pompey defeated the Jews and Israel became a tributary of Rome. In 20 BC Herod, the Great enlarged and beautified the Temple. This was the temple of Jesus' day.

Two political parties, not mentioned in the Old Testament but prominent in the New Testament, the Pharisees (conservatives) and the Sadducees (liberals) arose during the time of independence. Also, synagogues, meeting places to study the Old Testament Scriptures, came into being. Both Jesus and the Apostle Paul preached and taught in the synagogues.

Angels appeared on the fields of Bethlehem announcing the birth of Jesus.

The New Testament

The New Testament is made of 27 books including history, letters and prophecy.

The Four Gospel, (Matthew, Mark, Luke and John) tell the story of Jesus. Matthew, Mark and Luke are called the *synoptic* Gospels because they contain the same general summary of the events in Jesus' life. Most scholars believe that Mark wrote first, and Matthew and Luke had his outline available. For this reason, many of the stories are similar in content. John is more of a devotional Gospel and written much later. John not only records the history of Jesus but also focuses upon of his person and purpose.

The Book of Acts, written by Luke, presents the history of the first century Christian Church, beginning with the event of Pentecost. The first twelve chapters primarily speak of the development of the Church in Jerusalem. Beginning with chapter thirteen, the Apostle Paul and his ministry to the Gentiles takes center stage. Journey with Paul and his team. Get a map and traces his steps.

The Letters or Epistles, most written by the Apostle Paul, provide the earliest New Testament content. 1 Thessalonians was written as early as 55 or 56 AD. After preaching the Gospel in various cities and thus people became believers in Jesus, the Apostle would write to them a letter of teaching, correction and encouragement. There are also two letters of Peter, one of James and Jude and three of the Apostle John. The major share of Christian doctrine or teaching is drawn from these letters or epistles.

Imagine that these first Christian Churches continued to grow even though they had no trained clergy, no Bibles, no catechisms or material of any kind. Consider how eagerly they anticipated the letters from Paul and the other Apostles teaching them about Jesus. How fortune we are to have our Bibles and catechisms, and how unfortunate it is that few people read them.

The Book of Revelation presents the visions of the Apostle John while exiled on the Island of Patmos. The content is highly symbolic and open to numerous interpretations.

Here ends the New Testament.

The Starting Line

Recognizing your need for spiritual exercise, prepared to seek the enlightenment of the Holy Spirit, learning how to meditate upon the Word of God, and setting your priorities, where do you begin?

When often asked this question, I respond by saying, "Read Luke, Acts and Romans." If we were stranded on a dessert island and we had the Books of Luke, Acts and Romans with us, we would have everything we need for life and salvation.

Why Luke rather than Matthew, Mark or John? The Gospel of Luke and the Book of Acts were written by the same author – Luke. This is evident in the early verses of each document as they were addressed to the same person, a man by the name of Theophilus. They tell one story: the ministry of Jesus on earth and how He continued that ministry as the Holy Spirit was working through the Apostles.

When you read Luke and Acts, do not merely be an observer. Be a participant! Put yourself into the accounts. Be one of the shepherds on the fields of Bethlehem; be in the crowd when Jesus performed miracles; be in the upper room; in the Garden; on the streets of Jerusalem as Jesus passed by bearing His

Cross; stand beneath the Cross and behold the price paid for your sin; run with the women to the tomb; and join the disciples on the road to Emmaus as their eyes are opened to who Jesus is. Consider what your life would be like as a part of the early church. Think of the situation you would be in if you as a pagan heard the Apostle Paul preach the Gospel, and you came to faith. How would you tell others? Don't merely observe. Participate!

Meditate upon the teachings of Jesus. Personalize every promise. Listen carefully to the sermons preached in the Book of Acts. Be amazed when Gentiles who have no understanding of the Old Testament come to faith when Paul preaches the Gospel. Evaluate Paul's defense in the Book of Acts before King Agrippa.

The Book of Romans is the only epistle that present consecutive Christian truth - one truth built upon the preceding truth. The first eight chapters of Romans present many meaty verses that will require quiet meditation. Read and study these eight chapters very carefully verse by verse. Pray diligently for the Holy Spirit to open your eyes to the truth presented. Personalize every promise because they are for you.

After slowly and carefully reading Luke, Acts and Romans, continue with Galatians, Ephesians, Philippians and Colossians. Come to grips with the central teaching of justification by faith, understand what it means to be a part of the Church, learn to rejoice in the Lord always, and remember, everything is about Jesus.

For devotional purposes, before going to sleep at night, read one or two of the Psalms.

Whenever you come up with a question regarding some doctrine or teaching, the *Christian Cyclopedia* available on the Internet is a great source.

I encourage you to read Luke, Acts and Romans often. I also encourage you to begin the task of memorizing the Book of Romans, especially the first eight chapters. Here is what Martin Luther said about Romans: "This letter is truly the most important piece of the New Testament. It is purest Gospel. It is well worth a Christian's while not only to memorize it word for word but also to occupy himself with it daily. As though it were the daily bread of the soul. It is impossible to read or to meditate on this letter too much or too well. The more one deals with it, the more precious it becomes and the better it tastes."

I would encourage you to go out and buy yourself a brand-new Bible, possibly the *English Standard Version* or the *New International Version*. Buy one with a fine leather binding that feel good in your hands and cherish it. May God bless you in your daily workout with the Word of God.

Made in the USA
Monee, IL
02 August 2023

40334271R00059